J. EARL SHOAFF

"HOW TO BECOME A MILLIONAIRE"
OR
"HOW TO GET EVERYTHING YOU WANT OUT OF LIFE"
TRANSCRIPT

OVERVIEW

In this 1962 audio recording, you will hear the exact same presentation given by John Earl Shoaff that changed Jim Rohn's life and helped him become a millionaire within six years!

Aged 25, Jim was employed as a stock clerk at Sears taking home $57 a week. Married and with a family to support, Jim found himself falling behind with his bills. Like many of us, Jim knew that he wanted more out of life but had no idea back then how to make it happen.

Then something happened that changed Jim's his life forever. He attended a presentation given by Mr J. Earl Shoaff, also known as "The Millionaire Maker."

Speaking of the experience, Jim said: "To this day, I can't tell you exactly what he said, I just knew that I would have given anything to be like him."

Anyone who ever heard Jim Rohn speak, will be more than familiar with the impact that Earl Shoaff had on Jim's life.

You are about to hear the only known recording of the 1962 presentation, given by Earl Shoaff, that dramatically changed Jim's life and provided the secrets to his success. Needless to say, you are about to have a once in a lifetime experience! Enjoy and implement!

J. EARL SHOAFF
"HOW TO BECOME A MILLIONAIRE"
OR
"HOW TO GET EVERYTHING YOU WANT OUT OF LIFE"
TRANSCRIPT

INTRODUCTION
THE MILLIONAIRE MAKER.

The second greatest story ever told may well be the turning point in your life, regardless of your age. The voice you will hear on this recording is that of John Earl Shoaff, one of the most creative and inspired men of our time. Born with a weak heart and of modest means, his formal schooling did not go beyond the 9th grade.

During World War II he was rejected by the military because of this heart condition. Yet he joined the American Field Services overseas and, as an ambulance driver, and medical corps man, was in constant combat duty for over two years and this caused irreparable damage to his heart but it enkindled a determination to devote his remaining years to some service that would help man achieve greater fulfilment.

Starting as a pants presser after the war, he became a millionaire in less than four years and subsequently headed several large corporations with unprecedented success. He was intimately acquainted with the outstanding men of industry and government but never waivered in his drive to awaken men and women of all ages to their true potential. He frequently toured the country telling spellbound audiences that "Life never never withholds anything from anyone." Love, health, supply, companionship, employment. All these exist in infinite abundance. We are alone with one to prevent our own good from flowing simply because we are not aware of natures abundance and the tremendous power dormant in each of us. Power which unfortunately remains untapped because we don't know how to release and set in motion the activities which function these laws.

He felt one of life's great tragedies was mans persistence in clinging so tenaciously to lack and limitation The true mark of greatness is not just in what a man accomplishes himself but in his ability to help others help themselves and realise that they too can become great. John Earl Shoaff was such a man. But what is more, he had that rare ability of simplfying the laws of success and abundance to where even children understood and successfully applied them. Therein is the great value of this recording and why it can be the turning point in your life. However, your life will not change overnight by just hearing it once. Listen to it twice a day, every morning and evening, as you go about your daily chores and do what it says. And in one month, the most amazing things will begin happening to you and your family. Mr Shoaff used to say,

"Be naive enough to believe what I say for just 30 days and you will be on your way to a new life." That's why so many called him *"The Millionaire Maker."*

Recently a prominent Senator remarked, *"Had I owned this record 10 years ago, I would be in the White House today."*

In 1962, at the Essex House in New York City, Mr Shoaff was the key speaker at a large gathering of successful independent distributors from all over the United States. As we listen, he has just been introduced by the Master of Ceremonies.

I just want to take a few moments and cover some things that have assisted me in acquiring things in my life. I know that few people are aware of these basic fundamental laws that operate in this world of ours. Some people are aware of them; some people are not aware of them, but they are using them. And sometimes we wonder why certain things happen to us, we acquire certain things and then over a period of time it seems like we live in stagnation. Nothing happens; nothing takes place; everything seems to be at a standstill.

But there are basic laws in this universe that we are governed by and they work for you if you know how to apply them. And I would like to cover a couple of these laws just to assist you in knowing why these things happen. For an example, everybody is aware of the law of gravitation. Now, we do not know how it works, but we know it works. It works for everybody. It doesn't matter whether you are a saint or whether you are the opposite to a saint. If you jumped off a 20-storey building and you are a saint and you land on a concrete sidewalk, you are going to be an unhealthy saint. If you happen to be a crook and you do the same thing, the same thing happens to you. So basically, it doesn't matter whether you are good or bad. If you use the law of gravity wrong you are going to suffer.

The law of electricity works for all of us. If we use it properly, we can light our homes by screwing a light bulb into a socket. If we stick our finger into it, then we get bit. You're going to get burned. You can burn your house down with electricity or you can light your home with it. You can cook with it. You can use refrigeration. All the great things that electricity will do for us. You do not have

5

to be electrical minded person. You don't have to be a genius to do it. A child three years old can push a button and turn the lights on. And one of the first rules of the greatest electronic engineer in the world, all he can do when he pushes that button is turn the lights on too. So basically, it does not matter. The law of electricity will work for you.

We have laws of success. We have laws of poverty. We have laws of lack, laws of prosperity. We have laws of hate. We have laws of love. We have laws of peace. All of these are basic laws. If we use them rightfully, wonderful things will happen to us. If we use them wrong, then we get ourselves in trouble.

Now, one of the things that always has bothered me is, in all the books that I've ever read, on setting goals in life, positive thinking, positive goals that we want in life; and many of you people have probably read similar books; we follow these different steps, rules, laws, exactly and if we set 10 goals in life, we end up with 2. We lose out on 8. So it is not like the law of gravity seemingly, because it doesn't work every time. And the only reason it does not work every time, is because we do not use the right law. We are only using part of the law, and so the law of averages will give you a certain percentage of your goals. That is all. You say, *"Gee, wasn't that great? This happened to me."* But whatever happened to all the other goals you had in life? I'm going to lay down a simple basic way and you can have anything in this world you want to have and you can be anything in this world you want to be, and it's a simple basic situation. There's absolutely no problem to it. These are scientific things that work every time if you will do it in a simple way.

Now, the first thing that we want to become aware of is that we are going to be like farmers. We are going to plant seeds, and these seeds that we plant are the seeds we're going to reap. Now we are all aware that if you plant a seed of tomatoes, you are not going to get cucumbers; you're going to get tomatoes. If you plant a watermelon seed, you're not going to get grapefruit. You're not going to get radishes. If you want radishes folks, you must plant radishes. And when you plant a seed in the earth, you must plant it properly. And if you do not plant it properly, you will not have the harvest.

Now one of the major problems in our country today, for the average person, is they take the time and the effort to buy all the harvesting equipment, but they do not understand the planting and the cultivating. We want to reap harvest, but we do not want to take the time to plant, and we do not want to take the time to cultivate. Now the planting of the seeds, in the earth, is basically and absolutely the same process that you use in the mental world.

We are born with a conscious mind and a sub-conscious mind. We are the only animal in the kingdom that has both the conscious and the sub-conscious mind. A mind can decide at anytime in life where we want to go or what we want or what we don't want. We can decide with this conscious mind of ours, at any moment, whether we want to do a thing or if we don't want to do it. We can decide what we want to eat or if we don't want to eat. We can decide what we want to drink or what we don't want to drink. We can decide what we want in life, in a home, in an automobile, in the clothes we wear, the stove we buy, anything that we want in this world; any type of furniture, any type of a home, any type of an anything. We decide at anytime right here.

Now, where most people are making a mistake is they set their goals down. They say, *"Well, there's your goals, wri-*

te them down." So a fellow sits down, he says, *"I want a car, I want a house, I want some furniture, I want some new clothes, I want some money."* And this is the way they set their goals. Now folks, if we had a whole group of seeds, let's take apple seeds. We had 50 different types of apple seeds, and we just grabbed any one of them. We want apples. We throw them in the ground and they come up and they say *"Jeez those are green apples, I wanted red ones."* Well that's because you just picked any type of an apple seed. You didn't describe it. So we must learn to define.

Now, you've heard of the word *"visualizing"*. That you have to learn to visualize things. And when you visualize something, this is the thing you are going to bring into your life, if the visualization is strong enough. And we're always visualizing things in our life, but the tendency is to visualize negative situations. Now the reason for visualizing negative situations is because, folks let's not kid ourselves, we are living in a negative world. If I ask somebody, I say; *"By the way Joe, how are you feeling today?"* He says, *"Good, fine."* The next day I ask him how he feels, and he says, *"I feel terrible. I have had a pain in my stomach and I ache all over."* And he goes into a...you'd think he was an actor. He can describe a negative situation in his body so wonderful. But when he feels good, he just says, *"Fine."*

How come people, when they feel fine, they don't say, *"I feel great; I feel wonderful; I feel so great that I expect all the wonderful things in the world to happen to me today!"*? In other words, have a little feeling when you talk about the good things in life. I say, *"How are you doing in business?"* The guy says; *"Fine."* Now if he has a bad day, I say *"How are you doing?"* he says, *"Lousy. Oh, let me tell you this is a... we're just having a terrible time. Did you read that article the other day? It took me several hours to find it; but it was on the*

8

back page down at the bottom in fine print, but I located it."
People like negative things. They seem to vibrate with them. For some strange reason, they don't want things that are negative in their life, but they keep insisting on talking about them. And they can paint the most beautiful picture of lost and lack. Immediately I say, *"By the way, the internal..."* and everybody immediately starts shaking..."combustion." A guy says, *"You know what I thought you were going to say?"* And he starts creating pictures and he says; *"Oh by the way, I wonder about last year, what I did with that...you know, I wonder if they'll find that."* And immediately he says, *"I can see the guy coming in the door now. I wonder when he'll be here, what he'll look like?"* And he gets a beautiful picture. And the next thing you know, the guy is knocking on his door. He created the picture and he brought it into his life.

And the funny thing about creating things, folks: we are creators. Nothing comes to us. Everything comes through us, from us. Everything in this world that happens to us comes from here, not out here. And everything that you have in your life is exactly what you've designed. The dress you're wearing, the coat you're wearing, the tie you're wearing, the necklace you're wearing, the stole you're wearing, the home you're living in, the neighbors you've got, the friends you've got and the Senators you've got. So don't blame ME for people that you attracted!

When you signed this person up, you're the guy that coached him in. And you didn't care who he was as long as he come in. And pretty soon, you helped twenty of them and you say, *"You know what, Shoaff? I've got a lousy bunch of distributors."* Well, when you understand these laws, you won't tell me these things. Because you are basically saying, and I am not talking about you. I'm not talking about you. I wouldn't dare, there's too many here. So what I am saying is that everything we attract is what we are, and what I am speaks so loudly I cannot hear what you say. And what you are speaks so loudly I cannot hear what you say. You see, everything that you have is the things that you created. So be careful about what you create. Be careful. It's hard to visualize a thing.

By the way folks, let's visualize a 707, shall we? You guys say, *"What's a 707 look like? I've only been in one a couple of times. I've seen one up in the air once."* It's hard to visualize one. You want to visualize an automobile or a stole...or a... I don't know why I keep saying *"stoles."* My wife must be thinking of a stole. I keep getting that feeling. Every time we come to New York.

But you see, we have to learn to describe things. Now I'm going to go through a description of a thing because this is very important in your lives, folks. Please listen and please try to remember what I'm saying. You can change your life that quick and do everything wonderful; you can have everything wonderful happening to you, if you use these basic simple little things.

Now I'm going to describe a thing, an automobile. I'll talk about an automobile because an automobile is easy to describe, and people can comprehend it very quickly and very easily. And I'm not going to talk about a Chevrolet. I'm going to talk about a Cadillac. And anytime I'm talking about a Cadillac, folks, I'm not describing the Cadillac per se. I'm talking about a Cadillac idea. The Cadillac idea in the clothing, in the homes and the things you really desire deep within you. And I'm not talking about something that you say; *"Well, I've got to have money to have a Cadillac."* I'm not talking about money. It is not necessary that you have money to have a Cadillac. There's many wonderful things can happen to you, where these things can come to you from very unusual sources. Many wonderful things can happen to you. If you believe in the thing that I'm talking about; and if you can do and go through the process I'm talking about; your incomes will be doubled, tripled, quadrupled.

The one thing that I had in my mind, the first thing that I imagined that I had defined, imagine a pants presser, the one thing that I had in my mind , that I had defined in my mind, was a red Cadillac convertible. I never owned a Cadillac in my life. Now you probably don't want a red Cadillac. But I wanted one. And I defined that thing right down to its socks, and the end result was I had me a red Cadillac convertible, and my income increased to a point where it cost me nothing. This is visualizing. This is a positive attitude toward the things you want. Too many people stop their dreams because they start thinking about that thing that is not necessary in order to have it. I say to somebody, I say; *"Do you want a new Cadillac?"* The guy says, *"I want one, but I can't afford it."* I say, *"It has nothing to do with affording it this minute. I just want to know what you really want."* Most people are afraid to define what they want in life. They're afraid to define it. They're afraid it's going to cost them something. But if you're making $1,000 a month right now, and you could double your income to $2,000 a month, you could have your Cadillac, you could have two Cadillacs, you could have five Cadillacs. So you don't have to worry about the income. I'm just talking about a principle now. Now, the Cadillac. What do you do about it? I'll say, *"Pete, what would you like to have?"* He says, *"A Cadillac."* Now don't forget folks, I'm going to give it to him. I'm going to give it to him. So, he has nothing to worry about. No money, no nothing. So I says, *"Pete, what do you want?"* He says, *"A Cadillac."* I says, *"Fine, Pete."* Now this is wherepeoplemaketheirmistakes. Isay,"I'vegotanice1936beat-upmodel downstairs. I'll give it to

11

you." He says, *"I don't want a '36 model Cadillac."* I says, *"You just told me you wanted a Cadillac."* He says, *"I want a '62 Cadillac."* I said, *"Why didn't you tell me, Pete? Why didn't you tell me?"* This is the way people set their dreams. They just say *"I want a Cadillac."* Do you want an orange one or a green one? He says, *"I want a red one."* Now he's starting to define. And you know what, it's really difficult to define up here in your mind.

The first thing you do is to get a piece of paper folks and start defining on a piece of paper. A 1962 Cadillac; a red Cadillac; convertible. I'm just describing one car now. You can have any kind of car you want. A red Cadillac, 1962 convertible with a white top, red and white upholstering, a red floor rug, white wall tires, electric windows, air conditioning unit. The guy says, *"How much does that cost?"* I say, *"Don't worry about it, you're going to get it for nothing."* The guy says, *"I'll take it then."*

So now he says, *"I'm going to put everything down then, shouldn't I."* That's right. Describe it right down to the tee. So he goes right through this Cadillac and he describes it, everything about this Cadillac that he wants. And when he gets all through, the perfect visualization is up here now. Because he has described it. When you write it, you start seeing it. Because he says, lets see now, *"A Red Cadillac with a white top."* What color upholstering. Now he says, *"Lets see now. Red, all red. No, I'm going to have red with a white in it."* So he gets the picture up here by writing it down here. This is how you define things that you want in this world. So he gets it all defined. When he gets that Cadillac completely defined in his mind, he's got the seed. He hasn't planted it yet. He's got it picked out. Now the important thing is that you must release that seed. You must release it and it must be planted. And the finest thing in the world to plant that seed is to take on this piece of paper now and just write across that, *"Thank you".* That's the law of acceptance. And you would be amazed how many people in this world can't accept their goods. You would be shocked. *"Thank you"* means that I have accepted it. *"I'm going to have it. I know it's mine."*

And then you take and fold this piece of paper up with this goal on it, with this dream, your desire and you put it away. Put it underneath a tablecloth some place or put it in a drawer some place. Don't carry it around and don't take it out and look at it anymore. When you do this, that is planting it in the subconscious mind. You've accepted it, it goes into the subconscious mind, and the thing starts to work. Now the reason you put this away, the reason you put this seed away, after you have defined it, and the seed has been planted in the subconscious mind. You put it away some place, never to look at it again. And the reason for it, is like planting the seed in the earth, folks. If you go and dig that seed up two or three times a day to look at it, nothing's going to happen. And if you've ever seen a lack of faith, it's the farmer who had the gullibility to go and dig a seed up to find out if it was growing yet. Now this is real faith. He really believes in the laws of growth. And that's the same thing with us human beings. This is where we're making our mistakes. When we plant that seed in the subconscious mind, and it's there, the dream is there.

The thing starts working towards you. The Cadillac starts to work towards you. Events start taking place out here and the first thing you know it's getting closer and closer to you. Now if we take it out, and we look at it, the thing that happens is we say, *"I wonder where it's coming from."* This is a true showing of lack of faith. *"I wonder when it's coming."*" *I wonder how it's coming."* And so you are putting doubt into the law and it will not come folks. It will not come to you. Now, what's going to happen to the seed that you planted in the subconscious mind? You'll be driving down the street, you'll be in a restaurant talking to a friend and all of a sudden, there's a red Cadillac convertible with a white top and the whole thing will hit you right again and you'll see your dream. It'll keep coming back. The reason this thing keeps coming back to you, this is the only way that the universal law has of talking to you. There's no voice, it's all in visualization. And when this dream comes up, what it really means is that it is on its way to you. It is on its

way to you. It's right around the corner. And so you do not at that time say, *"How, when or where."* All you do is say, *"Thank you"* because you know it's on its way. And then immediately put it back out of your mind. Now how would you act if you really and truly wanted a red Cadillac convertible. If you really and truly wanted one. It was a strong desire in your life, and you knew it was on its way, how would you act? You'd be excited, wouldn't you? You'd feel good. You'd keep saying to yourself, *"Man it's almost here, it's almost here."* You'd walk taller, you'd look taller. You'd be happier. You'd be full of positive. You'd be more everything. And so you act different. You talk different. You even look like a prosperous person. You have things. Wonderful things are happening to you. Now, where does the positive attitude come in at? This automatically creates a positive attitude because it's the law of expectancy. Good things are going to happen. You have planted your seeds properly, and they are working themselves to you. And so you are automatically a positive person because all these wonderful things are going to happen.

Now, don't just have one seed planted, folks. Plant many seeds. Any great desire you have in your life, or tangible objects or intangible objects. You can have anything in this world you want to have and you can be anything in this world you want to be, by using this simple process. There is absolutely no way you can keep success from your door, if you will follow this basic, simple little process that I have just described. This is the law of life, and every one of you people have worked this process. But maybe you weren't completely aware of how you worked it. But think about it. That's why you only get 2 out of 8 things, or 3 out of 8, or 1 out of 8, or 1 out of 10, because you didn't know exactly the process that you were using. Now you know the process, so you can deal with anything in this world.

Children. Our children, folks. How many times have you heard people say to their children. The child says, *"I'm going to be President of The United States,"* and the father and mother will say to them, "You? With your studies, you'll never make it, Junior." Now this is a wonderful seed to plant in this fertile little brain. The subconscious little mind is putting in the mind. You're telling him he can't; he isn't smart enough. The child says, *"I'm going to be a rich man when I grow up. I'm going to have everything in this world."* You say, "You? You're going to have to learn a lot, Junior. One thing, you don't know how to handle money. You've got to learn to use that ol' elbow grease." Anybody who's ever used the elbow grease, I don't know has ever made millions, I'll assure you. The elbow grease is up here and very few people use that. Now, what do you want to tell Junior? Anytime any children come to you or to their parents, you should tell your children this and say; *"Junior, you're the type of child who can have anything in this world. You have the ability and the intelligence to go anywhere, do anything and have everything in this world. It is yours because you're that type of a child."* Start planting these seeds in

15

our children.

This country today is teaching too many children, too many children, what to think instead of how to think. And what are we? We are only children a little older than the other children. We are grown-up children, and we have to at some time in life, we have to start deciding and pinpointing things that we want in this world. And I am not just talking about the tangible objects. I'm talking about the intangible things. What would

you like to be? What type of person would you like to be? Would you like to have more love in your life? Well then, you must learn to give love. You'll never have anything without giving. Everything I give I receive back, multiplied. If I have a lot of hate in my life, I'm giving hate out. And so if I don't want hate coming in my life, I should not be giving it out. If I don't want people to talk about me, I shouldn't be talking about people. Everything that I send out, I get back...with feeling. Every thought I think I don't get, because I did not plant my seed properly. I did not have a true visualization.

How many of you ladies have thought of a beautiful dress or a beautiful something that you wanted to have. How many of you just said, *"I would love to have a mink stole"*? A few years ago, if my wife even mentioned a mink stole, the first thing that would come in my mind was, *"Well, where're you going to get it from? How are you going to pay for it?"* And I did not understand these things. When you just say, *"a mink stole,"* do you know what? I never was aware that there was so many mink stoles in the country. Every kind of every price and color and designs and everything else, and if you don't even know the exact kind you want, how do you ever expect to have it? Huh? It's like somebody saying. Do you know the amazing thing? The average person in this world, and I'm only saying this people because we are the average people of the world. And I say average because I am talking to an intelligent group of people. I'm not talking to the people way down the ladder. I'm talking to a group of intelligent people. And I'm saying this, and you analyze this yourself and ask yourself this basic question. Do you know what you want in life? If I was to ask you right now, *"What do you really want? What is a tangible object that you want in this world. The things that you can feel and touch and smell? What are these things that you want in life?"* And you know folks, the amazing thing? I doubt if there's 2% of the people in this room who could tell me and describe it, and just like that come right out and say it.

Because they have not been completely defined. I want a new home. I said what kind of home would you like? He says, *"Well, lets see now. Um, I think I'd like a 3 storey building."* Now this is a good way to pick your home. You think you'd like a 3 storey building. You don't know how many bedrooms? You haven't made out a design. You don't know exactly what you want. And this is why folks, that you know what happens? We get a lot of things that is left over from the people who know what they want. That's why we do not get the things, we haven't defined it. We do not know exactly what we want. How much success do you want? The guy says, *"I want a lot of money."* Let me tell you the importance in defining things. This is a very, very important thing. Very important. Boy you can get yourself messed up something awful if you don't follow this, properly.

A friend of mine, I told him about this idea of creating a vision, because when you get the vision of a Cadillac once more, you can even get the feeling of the thing. You can even see yourself in it. You can get the feeling of that thing. This is where things happen quick for you. I told this person about visualizing things, defining what he wanted. But he didn't define it completely. This was his dream. He wanted to take an ocean voyage. And he gets the feeling of the ocean voyage and everything else. He was in this ship, on the bow of the ship, you know, and the waves were rolling and the breeze was blowing in his face and the salt water was blowing in his face. And he had all the feeling and everything else. And within one year's time, this dream came back to him because he was standing on the bow of a ship. And the swell of the waves. And the breeze was blowing in his face and the salt water was hitting him on his face. But he forgot to define it completely and he was taking his voyage, he was in the service. Be sure and define your dream exact.

My niece, ever since she was born, she is now 20/21 years old. We have been teaching her these ideas. But you know people don't hear so good. They just hear what they want to hear, they for some strange reason you tell a guy "You want it? What do you want? You can have anything in the world you want to have. Anything. You name it. You can have anything ." And the guy says, *"Well, I haven't got the time to write it down."* Here you go, I say, *"If you dig a ditch from here to Washington DC, 6 feet deep, 3 feet wide, I'll give you a million dollars."* The guy gets a shovel and says, *"Right I'm digging."* But I say, *"I'll give it to you."* The guy says *"Yeah, ..."* Isn't that amazing?

My niece, we've been telling her this thing over and over and over. About visualizing and pinpointing the things that she wanted in her life. I says, "What do you want?" She says, "Money. Money." I says, "How much money?" She says, "Just big piles of money." So folks, she got this feeling, she could see it in her mind, piles of money, just counting out piles of it you know. Hundred dollar bills and fifties and coins and just money all over every place. And within 6 months time, within 6 months time, she was counting out money in a bank. She was a clerk in a bank. A cashier. She did not define it. Said it was her money she was counting. That's why these things are important. It's important to define things. Just like the fella says, I said *"What do you want?"* He said *"I want to earn $1000 a week."* I said, *"You'd better get a little bit closer to it than that buster. You're not defining it."* He said, "What's wrong with that?" I says, *"Well, I know a lot of people that are earning a $1000 a week and they're only getting..."* So you want to say,*"I want to earn and I want to receive a $1000 a week."* Now, there's one thing about the sub- conscious mind folks. It does not play favorites. It doesn't kid. It doesn't fool. And everything that you plant there you're going to reap. That's why you want to be sure that you plant exactly what you want. That's why people are getting all the time things that they don't want. A guy says, *"I want a house."* So he gets a house, any kind of a house, but he gets it. *"How come I get a house like this? This isn't exactly what we wanted. We'vebeeninhere3months.Weshouldhavehad3bedroomsinsteadof2."* Andhe says, *"How come we got this?"* He didn't know what he wanted so he just got a house. He didn't define it. He wouldn't have had that house if he had defined it. And so that is what everything in this world. Everything. If you want to be a happier person, define the type of person that you would like to be. Define it. Pinpoint it. Write it down. Write across there, "thank you." Plant it deeply. And once you did, don't worry about it anymore. This is going to happen to you. All wonderful things are going to happen to you to make you a happy person.

You want more success. How much success? You know, when I was working in the dry clean business I was making a 100 bucks a week, less than a 100 bucks. You know what happened? A $100 a week. If somebody had told me that they would pay me $200 a week I would have said, *"Oh Man."* This is the end. This is the end. I could retire practically on $200 a week. So what is success? What is success? If I talk to a man who's making $3000 a month and told him I was going to pay him $200 a week, he wouldn't be very happy about the situation.

So, what is success in your life? What is it that you want? Define it. Write it down. Pinpoint every drop of that dream that you have in your mind. Define it so clearly on that piece of paper that you can completely see it in your mind. And when you get it written down, write *"thank you"* on it and plant that seed and put it away, and it will start to materialize and it will start coming into your life. That is anything folks, anything, anything.

Now a guy says, *"I'm going to put down The Statler Hotel."* You know why it wouldn't work for him? You know why it wouldn't work for him? I'm not saying it won't work for the fellow, but I am saying that it won't work for the average person. Do you know why? He couldn't even imagine getting it. He can write it down. He can define it, and he can put *"thank you"* on it, but he can never plant the seed. And the reason he can't is because he couldn't even imagine getting The Statler Hotel, that's why. And don't forget, this is something that you have to accept. You're going to have it, folks.

I told people about a Cadillac, the average people working on average jobs. I said, *"Do you want a Cadillac?"* The guys said, *"Well, no, I don't want no Cadillac."* I said, *"Well, why don't you want a Cadillac?"* He said, *"Well, for one thing, it costs so much to operate them."* You see, he doesn't want one. He isn't ready for that step yet. Now say he steps from one car to another to another. He raises his consciousness, until pretty soon he can buy Cadillacs like the average guy buys a pair of shoes. And you can grow. You can grow inyourthinking. I'vehadpeoplesay, "Boy,yougotto-becarefulaboutpeople.Youknow they'll take you in if you're not careful." And they get such a wonderful visualization, they're always getting taken in. And so you see how we build these pictures in our minds? People will spend the morning; they're going to get ready for a wonderful day. Tomorrow morning now, we're getting ready for a wonderful day; we're going out and it's going to be the most successful day we've ever had in our entire life. I said, *"How are you going to start the morning? Exactly what are you going to do?"* He says, *"Well, the first thing I'm going to do is I am going to go out on the porch."* He's going through his morning now. He's going out on the porch and he's going to get his newspaper and read a little bit about positive thinking in the headlines. And if he can't find it there, he'll look and look and look and look until he finds something that is really good and negative and then he'll tell his wife and describe it. He says, *"Guess what I found in the paper?"* And he starts telling her about some wonderful divorce that's taken place and the kids committed suicide, and he'll go on with this and he'll say, *"Just imagine that, imagine what's happening here!"* And he'll describe it, and he'll describe it and he'll go on with his negativity and the negativity will get started and the wife will get negative and he will get more negative and when he gets all through with breakfast now, he's in such a nasty mood that he don't even like his dog! And he's going out to face the world with a positive attitude. Do you see how ridiculous it is folks? Do you see how ridiculous it is and some of the ridiculous things we do in life and we wonder why success doesn't always come to us in the proportion that we'd like to have it come to us?

Expect wonderful things. Be a creator of ideas. Let's not be moons, the reflector of ideas. Let's be suns, let's be the creator of the light; let's be the creator of the ideas, because we all have a capacity. You know that the guardian of the gate, as the conscious mind. This guardian can at any time let any thought through to the subconscious mind it wants. Any thought at any time. We are thinking human beings. We have the capacity to think of anything, anything in this world we can think of, but we do not have the capacity to think of nothing. Now you try to imagine what nothing is. Try to get a thought of that. There is absolutely no way. So that means that we are thinking human beings and there are thoughts flying through our mind continuously. A steady flow of thoughts all the time coming through the mind. Now where do these thoughts come from? Allofasudden, yousay, "Gee, thatthoughtmusthavecomeoutoftheclearblue sky. It must have come out of the clear blue to me." You didn't think of it, in fact it might have been something you didn't even know about. And the thought comes through and you say, "Well, that's kind of ridiculous, isn't it? That couldn't happen to me." And so you throw that thought aside. And if it's a good thought, why not accept it? And stop and analyze it and accept it. And let them happen to you. And these objects coming through to you all the time. But a negative thought comes through and it stops there and you say, "Boy, that's a good negative thought. I'll stop and memorize that one." And you start thinking about it and pretty soon you get a frown on your face and you think about it a little bit more and you create a beautiful picture and all of a sudden you put that down in the subconscious and you say, "Well, there's another bad thing that's going to happen to me." Have you ever caught yourself thinking about something you didn't want to think about and you've been thinking about it for

22

5 minutes and all of a sudden you think, *"What am I thinking about that nasty thing for?"* We do it. We do it all the time, folks. But we can stop now, any time we want. And we can change that thought and put in a good thought.

If you don't want to think about oranges, change the thought and think about bananas, if you want. If you don't want to think about lack, change the thought and think about prosperity. If you don't want to think about hate, think about love. If you don't want to think of anything that is negative, put a positive idea in your head. You know what happens, you can analyze it and you can just dream about it and everything else, and get all these seeds planted properly and have all these wonderful things happen. Get twenty wonderful seeds planted, get them written down. Define. Thank you. Plant them into the subconscious mind. Put it away, and every time it comes back into the mind and the law is saying it's on its way, you just say *"Thank you."* Don't analyze it because it's already planted. Just say "Thank you" and go on. And have ten, fifteen, twenty, thirty of these wonderful seeds planted and folks, you'll walk on air. And you'll have miracles happen in your life. And don't be afraid to do this.

Your wife isn't in harmony with the wonderful things that you want to happen to you; well, if the husband isn't in harmony with you or if the children aren't, or your friends aren't, you don't have to show them. Plant your seeds privately then, and put them away privately and plant them deep and all these wonderful things will happen and you'll say, *"You know, one thing about that person, I don't know what happened to him, but man oh man, everything they touch turns to gold."* And that's the reason. That's the reason, folks. The planting properly of your seeds.

It's a real pleasure being here with you. Thank you very much.

Recommended Readings

- Warren Buffett Talks to MBA Students by Warren Buffett

- Monetary Policy Alternatives at the Zero Bound: An Empirical Assessment (Finance and Economics Discussion) by Ben S. Bernanke

- You Can Still Make It In The Market by Nicolas Darvas

- The Richest Man in Babylon - Illustrated by George S. Clason

- Invest like a Billionaire: If you are not watching the best investor in the world, who are you watching?

- Back to School: Question & Answer Session with Business Students by Warren Buffett

- New Trader, Rich Trader: How to Make Money in the Stock Market by Steve Burns

Available at www.bnpublishing.com